EXCITING LIFE *of* JOE SORENSON

JOE SORENSON

ISBN
978-1-961358-81-2 (Paperback)
978-1-961358-82-9 (eBook)

TABLE OF CONTENTS

INTRODUCTION

Hi, this is Joe Sorenson. Would you like to take a trip in time through a life's journey? I have just the one for you. So, fasten your seat belts, and let's take a ride.

Exciting Life of Joe Sorenson

In *Exciting Life of Joe Sorenson*, Joe Sorenson masterfully narrates his personal stories and shares introspective poems, inviting readers to join him on a journey through the various stages of his life. He sheds light on his childhood struggle with an eye defect, detailing a treatment that left him with limited vision in his left eye and complete blindness in his right. Despite this significant challenge, Joe pursued a life of his own choosing with unwavering determination. Growing up in Saint Paul, Minnesota, Joe left home at 24 and moved to Worthington, Minnesota, in 1966 to live independently. His subsequent tales delve into his career choices and relationships, painting a vivid picture of his life's milestones. From operating a retail stand in a post office to securing his dream job, falling in love, and enduring heart-wrenching loss, Joe's stories are both compelling and inspiring.

I found Joe's lyrical and engaging book thoroughly enjoyable. His poems and remembrances are rich with deep reflections and provoke thoughtful contemplation on life's diverse experiences. Some poems are personal tributes, such as "A Tribute to My Dad" and a heartfelt homage to his mentally ill brother, Peter. Others explore various subjects, including mornings, learning braille, and the institution of marriage.

Exciting Life of Joe Sorenson captivates from start to finish, with Joe's evocative experiences and relationships taking center stage. Despite their brevity, his recollections form a rich tapestry of intriguing themes that resonate deeply. For instance, his account of a long-distance relationship and the resulting heartbreak reminded me of my own similar experiences, sparking a profound connection with his writing. Joe emerges as an inspiring figure with an upbeat personality, undeterred by life's challenges. His relentless pursuit of his dream job in radio and his efforts to sustain love despite distance showcase his remarkable determination. The author's cheerful and expressive writing style, combined with his impressive acts of resilience, make this book an inspiring and energizing read.

Exciting Life of Joe Sorenson is a must-read for anyone who appreciates stories that highlight the importance of cherishing love, and family, and following one's dreams. Joe Sorenson's life is a testament to the power of perseverance and the beauty of living authentically, making this book an unforgettable experience.

1

BIRTH

Drama in the Hospital

In 1941, in the month of August, there was excitement at Midway Hospital in Saint Paul, Minnesota. A baby was born. I weighed eight pounds and had brown hair. This was no ordinary baby. This is what they tell me. How did I know? When I popped out, the chord was wrapped around my eyes. This was an unusual birth defect. That left me totally blind.

That scared the staff and my parents. They did not know what to do. So they searched for a doctor who could try to help this child to see. They found such a man in Dr. Frank Burch who knew how to tackle such cases. He agreed to try. I am only writing what I have been told. I was too young.

Because of my mother's deep faith, I was named Joseph, the one who was sold as a slave, but he rose to the top.

Here is a little poem about Joseph:

Joseph, Joseph—
you were sold as a slave
and went through the mill

and climbed the hill
to the top
and prospered.

This is what I was told. At ten days old, Dr. Burch did the first surgery at Miller Hospital in Saint Paul, Minnesota. Dr. Burch was scared to do it, but he tried it anyway. If any eye doctor could tell me how one could measure such eyesight at that age, please tell me. This left me with a little sight, which I still have in my left eye but none in my right eye. In my left eye, I can see bright colors, light, and some objects up close. In fact, I don't have an eye on the right. During this time, I had thirteen eye operations by the time I was five years old.

Here is another poem:

With Partial Sight

Oh my, I can see,
with glee,
the color red,
the sun,
the clouds,
lights—
the white, white snow!
Oh my, the faces
up close
like my wife
and my mother who is in heaven.
All kinds of flashlights,
lightning from thunderstorms—
oh, what a flash!

Now I can tell you what I remember. In my toddler years of two and three, I was rushed into the operating room, kicking and screaming, "I want my mommy!" The staff tried to keep me quiet, but it didn't work. I screamed even louder, "I want my mommy!" They even tried to bribe me with the promise of ice cream. But did it work? No. The only thing that would shut me up was the anesthetic ether.

Even my brother, Peter, who was a year and a half older, teased me with all the bandages on my eyes, saying, "It looks like you have been in a war."

2

⸺ ◆◆◆ ⸺

PUBLIC SCHOOL

I bet you want to know where this kid went to school. This is hard to believe, but it is true. This is not a lie.

On a hot summer day, when I was four years old at home, there was a knock on the door. I had no idea who it was. It turned out to be the superintendent of the Minnesota Braille and Sight Saving School (now the Minnesota State Academy for the Blind) in Faribault, Minnesota, which is about fifty-five miles away from Saint Paul, Minnesota.

He wanted to talk to my parents about the school and all the things that their son could learn. There was a big discussion about this, and after some deep thought, my parents said no and kept me home.

The Sandbox Years

This may sound strange to you, but it did happen. My parents sent me to the Saint Paul Public School in Saint Paul, Minnesota. The school promised to teach me braille. Did they keep it? No. My parents agreed.

I was happy to be a normal kid and play like the sighted kids do. Here is the strange part. The first year was kindergarten at Gordon School. I was five years old. This was easy. Any kid can flunk kindergarten!

On September 2, 1947, I went to first grade at Hill School, in Saint Paul, Minnesota. I was six years old. I was supposed to start learning braille then.

There was not a teacher who could teach me. In fact, I was the only blind kid in the class. This is hard to believe, but this is due to the fact that in those days there was only one teacher for multiple grades.

The classroom was much like any other classroom, with one window and desks and a blackboard in front. The bathroom was in the basement. The other kids needed to guide me back and forth at first. Then I knew where I was going. They put me in a corner with a sandbox to play in. It was a large, square box with white sand in it and different toys to play with. One of the toys was a ball.

One day, I lost the ball, and another kid found it and gave it back to me. The only time that I was allowed out of the box was to have lunch at a desk and to listen at 11:00 a.m. on radio station KUOM, the Minnesota School of the Air. Later in life, I worked there as a student announcer. This was a struggle, but I will talk about it later.

I got an education all right, in my imagination. I had lots of fun. This went on for two years. Can you imagine what that does to a child's brain? It almost happened to me.

Here's another poem:

The Sandbox

Most sandboxes are outside,
but this one was inside.
Oh my, the white sand
with all the toys
to play with,
so much fun—
the stories that I can make up
in the sandbox!

One day in 1948, when I was seven years old, my dad came home from work with a braille book in his hands. I was upstairs in my room. This was a two-story home. I was glad to see my dad, but I was scared because I couldn't read at that time. He wanted to know if I was learning anything. So he asked me to read something from the book. I couldn't.

So he asked the question, "What do you do all day?"I froze. Tuffy the cat took my tongue—*ouch*.

Finally, after a long time, I told him. He was mad.

Here's one more poem:

My Dad

Oh my,
How mad he was
that I couldn't read!
He raised his voice,
not at me,
but at the school.

I almost became mentally ill like my brother Peter.
And now, here are a few more poems that my wife Ellen and I wrote. These will make you laugh.

Work Order

Plumbing,
lights, flooring,
and more—
these are the things
that can go wrong
when you live in an apartment.
When you call the office,
and make your request,

you get this answer:
"Work order."This happens every time
You request for help.
There are times
when you wait
in the dark
with no water,
so all you have
at that time
to keep you company,
is the TV.
However,
if the lights go out,
you don't have the TV either,
so the only thing you could possibly have
is a portable radio and a flashlight
or candles or your cell phone.

* * * * *

To My Mom
A Tribute to My Mother

In the month of May,
in the year 1984,
my mother was in hospice,
in Saint Paul, Minnesota,
traveling
on a slow train to heaven.
On Sunday afternoon,
the day before
Memorial Day,

she lost
her power of speech;
however, she was smiling
because she heard my voice on the radio
spinning
gospel music, on radio station KUXL.
Now I know
she is smiling, and singing, and shouting
in heaven.

* * * * *

Prayer

Do you lack power in your life?
Moments of discouragement will disappear—
Jesus is waiting to hear from you.
All you have to do
is talk to him.
All that it takes is a little time,
and your bucket of cares will
disappear.
This is what prayer is all about—
a conversation with God.

* * * * *

Dad
A Tribute to My Dad

My dad was a kind and loving
person who put his heart
into what he did.
He was not musically inclined;
however,
he loved to
open the hymnbook
and make a joyful noise.
It was not pleasing to human ears,
but the angels loved it,
the Lord was glorified by it.

* * * *

Resurrection

Fear not—
do not despair.
Why do you look so sad?
Rejoice and be glad,
Jesus Christ
is risen today!
So let us all celebrate,
with a joyful sound,
to the Glory of God.

* * * *

Martin

Courage,
strength,
determination,
honor, and faith—
these features describe
Dr. Martin Luther King Jr.
This man we all know and honor,
this is a little-known fact
about his
"I have a Dream" speech.
It was delivered on August 28,
in the year 1963,
on the steps of the Lincoln
Memorial in Washington, DC.
He did not want to talk about his dream;
however, Mahalia Jackson,
behind the podium, said,
"Martin, tell them about the dream."
So the great leader
was shot down
on April 4, 1968.
He will always be remembered
forever
and ever.

* * * *

Morning

Up in the morning,
it comes without warning;
please don't weep—
you've had a great sleep.
It is time to rise and shine and give
God the glory.
Come to Him in prayer and share your worldly cares;
it is time to study His word,
and He will give you
His divine power,
every minute and every hour.

* * * * *

Why I Love Classical Music
A Tribute to my Mother

Growing up in Saint Paul, Minnesota,
with my Mother, who was a great lady,
she always loved classical music—
I didn't at that time.
Every Saturday afternoon, she would listen
to the Metropolitan Opera broadcast
on the radio and bake cookies;
they were chocolate.
I liked top 40 music;
while the music of one of
Wagner's operas was flowing along,
I would float outside.
When I reached the age of twenty-four,

I began to see the light.
I love it now; for example:
the music of Wagner—
Lohengrin is one of my favorite operas.
Schubert and his love songs are thrilling.
I can't forget Tchaikovsky's
The *Nutcracker* ballet.
Handel's water music is constantly swimming.
There are lots more that I could talk about,
but that will come later.

* * * * *

Turning On the Lights

It is time to turn on the lights
for those in need.
Who don't have lights to turn on right now?
It is a time to spread some
Christian cheer,
so let us light up this little part of the world.

* * * * *

Tribute to Peter

Peter, Peter—you were a great leader,
just like any child, you loved nursery rhymes.
One of them is "Simple Simon."
At Christmastime, you loved the music;
you would say, "Christ the Lord."
When you became an adult,
you set the pace for others;
For example, when our cousin was little,
he wanted to pace the floor,
just like you.
At the group home, everyone loved you;
but now you are loved in heaven.

Do you really want to know what is next?

3

AND NOW, THE REST OF THE STORY

When I left off, I told my dad that I could not read the braille book that he brought home. I had no choice but to finish out that school year. In the autumn of the year 1949, I was off to the Minnesota Braille and Sight Saving School in Faribault, Minnesota. After two years of playing in the sandbox at Hill School in Saint Paul, I passed with the grade of an A. Why? I don't know. The sandbox was taken away.

Goodbye, Sandbox

Goodbye, sandbox—
It was nice knowing you.
It was fun to play in you!
You helped me develop my imagination.
My friends were sad to see me go, but they understood.

4

AWAY TO SCHOOL

In September 5th, 1949, I went off to school in Faribault. I was scared to go to a strange place where I knew no one. The only people I knew were my parents. One of the first places that I went to was the school hospital. I had to get weighed. The room was a typical exam room with an exam table, cabinets, a sink, a trash can, one window, and the scale that I stood on. When I got on the scale, it shook. It was not because I was fat—I was not—and it just didn't know me. I only weighed fifty-two pounds.

That night, I was in my room with three other boys. It was a large room with four beds, two on each side of the room, two dressers on each side, and two windows. I was in bed and trying to sleep, but I couldn't because I was scared and homesick. That didn't last long.

The next morning, we were at an assembly that was in a big room with a stage, soft chairs in two rows of ten in a row, and a walkway in the middle. There was a window in the back of the room. We were told that there were 130 of us.

130 of Us

Don't make a fuss—
there are only 130 of us.
I was shaking in my little shoes.

5

❖◆❖

BASKET CASE

When I got to my classroom, I was lost. I had to go back to kindergarten because I couldn't read, thanks to the "sandbox years." That was after the teacher noticed that I was not at the same pace with the other kids in the first grade. For example, when the bell rang, I didn't know that I needed to go to another class. The other kids thought that I was deaf or something, but I was not. I just didn't know what to do.

The rest of that year, I was in kindergarten. The room was a big room with a few desks, rugs on the floor, three windows, and some toys to play with. The bathroom was in the hall. I actually learned something that year. The day was split in to two parts, with a break for lunch and to listen to the radio. The soap operas were on at that time.

Soap Operas

Swimming, not with water and soap,
but with the radio
and to my joy.
On WCCO,
There was *The Second Mrs. Burton*,
then at 1:15 p.m., there was *Parry Mason*,
and at 1:30 p.m., *This Is Nora Drake*,

and then the bell rang.
I dried out; it all came out in the wash;
and I knew to go back to class.
At the end of the school year, I went home.

6

❖◆❖

SUMMERTIME

Do you remember when you were in school and summer came and you were happy to play all day? Well, I had to work during the hot days. My parents got some braille flash cards for me to learn with. They were small cards with words in braille on them. And I was instructed to practice, with my mother's supervision. I was not happy about that because I wanted to play like the other kids during the summer.

Learning Braille

Do you remember when you were taking piano lessons
and you had to practice at home?
Well,
I had to do just that—
except that it was with braille.
Learning braille, learning braille—
do not fail:
you are learning braille.

7

FIRST GRADE

In fall 1950, I went to the first grade at nine years old. We had a small room with small desks for the kids, the teacher's big desk, and one window in the back. There were about ten of us. I was to start learning braille at that time. Little did the teacher know that I had already started. To me, it was easy because I already knew the alphabet. That year, I earned the A that I got.

The rest of my time at the school was a breeze. I have to thank them for getting me out of my shell. If it weren't for them, I don't know where I would be now. For example, I did some dramatic readings, and I was in the school band playing trumpet. I sang in the school chorus. I also read from a braille hymnbook. I graduated in 1962.

Singing with a Braille Hymnbook

Singing, singing
with a braille hymnbook—
singing, singing
to the glory of God,
making a joyful noise unto the Lord!

8

♦♦◆♦♦

WORK LIFE

Shortly after I graduated, I went back home. The first job that I had was self-employment, doing door-to-door sales selling greeting cards and other small items. My dad would help me. He was the wheelman driving me where I needed to go. That lasted for about four years. Then I went into the Stand program.

In March 13, 1966, I left home at twenty-four years of age and moved to Worthington, Minnesota, which was about 180 miles from Minneapolis. It is a small town with a post office, some stores, and a hotel, which was where I lived. I opened a stand in the post office. It was in the corner. I sold candy bars and cigarettes.

On My Own

On my own, on my own,
Traveling with my white cane,
Even though I am blind,
I could go where I wanted to go
Without help.

During my time working at the stand in the post office, I resumed contact with the girl whom I ran into at school. Yes, I physically ran into her when I was still a kid. Her name was Virginia Rachael "Ginny" Cleeberger. She was born in 1929. She was short, about five feet two, with short, dark hair. She did not like her own last name. The kids called her "Cleeberger cheeseburger." The friendship grew, and we started dating.

It was long distance because of the miles between us. The first time that I saw her after our school days was in August 1966 in Minneapolis for a weekend. I continued to work in Worthington until December 1966. I had an opportunity to move up in the Stand program to a bigger stand in Saint Paul. I took it. That gave me the chance to be closer to Ginny. Are you ready for this?

On January 3 the next year, I moved back to Saint Paul to take the bigger stand at the old federal courts building. I had a whole room to myself. That was better because I could sell more stuff like tobacco products, candy bars, magazines, ice cream, and milk.

Love Story

Too far away from my love,
like a dove,
it broke my heart.
And what came in the mail
was an opportunity to move
closer to my Ginny,
so I took it happily.

9

---•◆•◆•◆•---

ENGAGEMENT

In a bright, sunny Sunday afternoon in June 1967, I asked Ginny to be my wife. We knelt down and prayed, and she said yes. We got married on October 21, 1967, at a small Methodist church in Northfield, Minnesota.

I worked in the Stand program until December 1969. During my time there, I did some dramatic readings at North Western College Radio. I had to resign from the Stand program for health reasons. My boss didn't like that. He was frustrated.

Marriage

Marriage, marriage,
It's better than a carriage,
It was meant to be,
The Lord put us together
Until the end.

10

◆◆ ◆ ◆◆

University and Radio Life

In spring 1972, I took a class at the University of Minnesota that was Introduction to Broadcasting. I found out that I could operate a control board.

Turning Point

I always wanted to work in radio—
when I was a child, I would make up radio shows,
for example,
The Lone Ranger.
I was told by broadcasting schools,
"No, you are blind,
you can't do that."
I showed them.

11

—◆◆◆◆·—

Announcing at First Covenant Church Radio

The services at 11:00 a.m. at First Covenant Church were carried on several stations in Minneapolis, as well as Nome, Alaska. In early 1974, there was an opening for an announcing job. I expressed my interest in announcing, and I supplied a tape. I went up to the radio room and talked to the crew. They were slow in saying yes. In fact, I had given up.

One evening, Dave and Sue who were heads of the radio room came to visit us at our home. David said, "When are you going to start announcing?" I said, "I have given up," and he said, "We are going to get you in there." On Wednesday night, I got the script for the Sunday service. I went on live the next Sunday morning. The pastor was mad.

On Monday morning at a phone booth and a dime in my shaking hand, I called the choir director and head of broadcasting. He said, "It is not that we don't want you. Can you come in on Wednesday evening at 6:15 p.m. to talk?" I said yes. I was shaking when I went in to talk. We talked, and I was hired. Later on, the pastor was so happy with the job that I did.

I had the desire to work at KUOM radio as a student announcer, but I had to work for it. The station manager was reluctant to have a blind person work there at first. She was away at a conference in Washington,

DC. You know the saying "When the cat's away, the mice will play"? Well, it happened.

While I was learning how to operate the board, I was about to pack up and go home because the station was about to go on the air at 10:30 a.m. At 10:25 a.m., the chief announcer asked me if I would like to go on at 10:30 a.m. I was scared and excited at the same time. I was ready, though. The person who was supposed to go on came in to work, but she was told, "Joe was going on but you are to be in there with him." That was fine with her. She was about to graduate from college anyway. I signed on and did my thing. I was hired there in June 1975 and worked there until 1977.

12

◆◆◆◆◆

SOUL GOSPEL MUSIC RADIO

You might want to know what I did next. Well, I will tell you. I became interested in soul gospel music. I prayed about it, and while shaking in my shoes, I called the station manager of radio station KMOJ. I came in to talk to her. She was nice. The station was located in a house. The studio was upstairs on the second floor. She had no problem having a blind person work there. I was pushed in the deep water right away without drowning.

During my time there, I was on the air six days a week. People would call in with requests, such as James Cleveland. There was a nice nine-minute song called "Please Be Patient with Me." There was one lady who called in and asked to hear that song over and over. She called and demanded to hear it by asking in an angry tone, "When are you going to play 'Please Be Patient with Me!'" Silence is golden because I said nothing.

During that time, I went back and forth, off and on, between two stations, KMOJ and KUXL, which was located in Golden Valley, Minnesota. On Sunday nights at 11:00 p.m., I was on the air playing soul gospel music. I had to get my own advertisers. During the week, they played CCM, which is contemporary Christian music. During the week, the listeners didn't hear music like Vanessa Bell Armstrong.

One time at KUXL, during the week, they invited listeners to call in with their questions about music. To my surprise, one phone call after another asked, "Why can't Joe Sorenson be on earlier?" The phone staff were silenced. There were about eight calls with that question. Those who answered the phone didn't know what to do.

Also, during that same time, there was a salesman who was a legally blind person who wanted to keep the place looking nice. His name was Mike. He saw a spot on the wall and wanted to get it off, so he tried. The station manager saw what he was doing and said, "Mike, you're a salesman here." Mike didn't know if he got the spot off. So he asked, "Is it coming off?" We will never know if it came off. I worked like that until 1991.

Then I had a chance to do a show at KNOF, but I had to buy the time to do my show, so I did sales to pay for my airtime. At that same time, I worked at WTCN, which was located in Stillwater, Minnesota. I did sales work and also my own gospel show. I was there for about a year. That lasted until 2004. You may ask, "How could you do all of that?" It was like a sandwich with radio in the middle. I started *Expressions of Joy*, which is a phone line in 2004.

Ellen stepped in to the picture at that time she was born in Alamogordo, New Mexico. She was a twin, but her sister didn't survive. She is short, about five feet three, and has straight short, brown hair and hazel eyes. She is in a wheelchair and is legally blind. Ellen, Ginny, and I became good friends. Ellen was in Albuquerque, New Mexico, at that time.

The first time that the three of us met was in March 2005 when we came to visit for her birthday. Then we met once more in July 2005 at a blind convention. We shared a room to save money. That worked well. Ginny and I were wanting to move out of our high-rent apartment, so in November 2005, we went to Albuquerque to look for housing. Ginny and I moved out to Albuquerque in April 2006.

In 2008, Ellen and I had a soul gospel radio show at 1550 on the AM dial. This was a local show. That didn't last long because we had to pay for the time. We searched for the lowest cost, and that was it. It was at 6:00 a.m. for an hour. We had to shut it down because we went broke.

13

CAREGIVING

My wife Ginny's health started going downhill after we moved. It was slow at first. In 2009, we had to get a wheelchair for her because of her balance and memory problems due to age. That year, she was put on home hospice. It was not because she was going to leave this world soon; it was for her safety.

It took a team to take care of her. Ellen also was a big part of the team. She helped with the housework and other stuff. This lasted until December 17, 2014, when we had to put Ginny into assisted living. That was for the last four months of her life. She went to heaven on April 30, 2015. We were married for forty-seven years. She was eighty-five years old when she went home to heaven.

Ellen loved Ginny like a sister. Sometimes when the two of them were doing things together, people would get them mixed up. People would also ask Ellen if Ginny was her mother because of the age difference. Ellen would say, "No we are good friends."

I was on my own for about five months, and I enjoyed it. That was until I asked Ellen to be my wife. It was on October 3, 2015, at the balloon park, with iced coffee in hand. The sun was out, and there were people all around. She said yes.

We got married on June 4, 2016. The ceremony was at the church that we were going to at that time. That was New Hope Full Gospel Baptist Church. When we left to get on the sun van to go to the hotel, the sun was shining, and we were followed by bubbles provided by our friend Nancy. We couldn't tell which was which.

Going to Heaven

Ginny, Ginny—
you stepped into eternity.
And now,
you are singing with the angels,
to the glory of God.

*   *   *   *

Fireworks

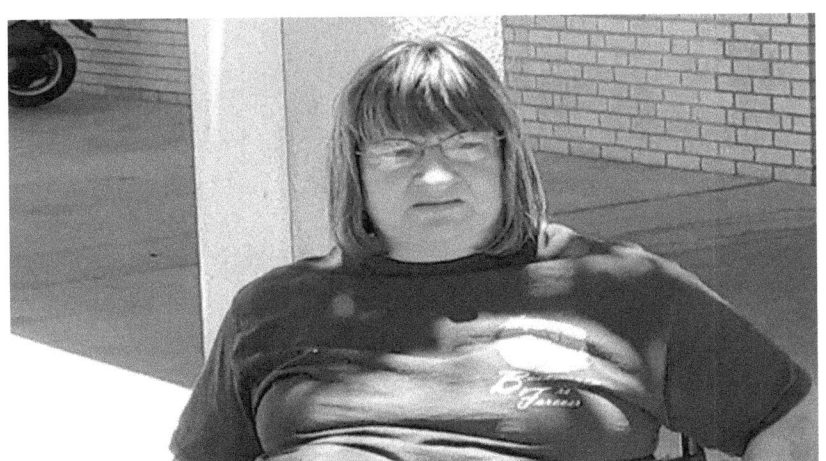

Oh Ellen, oh Ellen—
you are such a spark.
When you said yes to marriage,
you set off the fireworks.
What a bang!

*   *   *   *

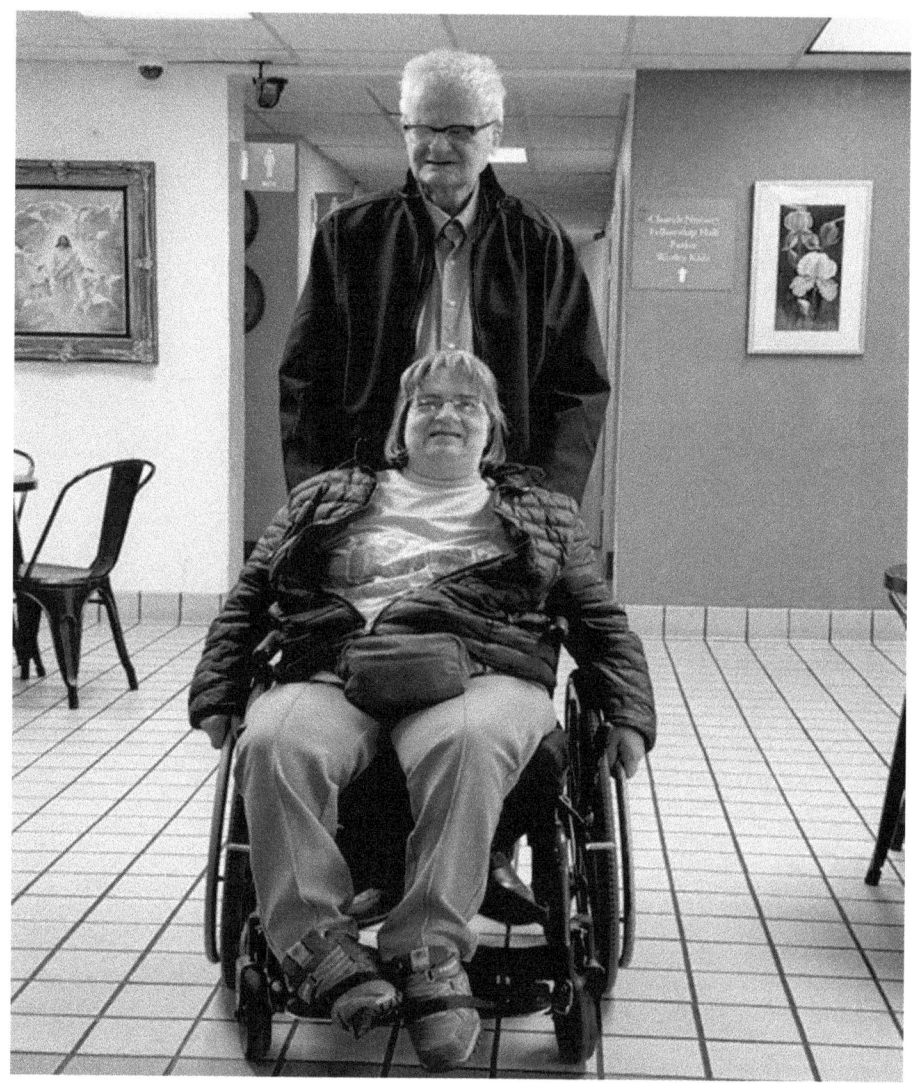

Ellen, My Wife

Ellen, Ellen, you are my beautiful wife,
what a bright June bride by my side!
We travel along with my hand on your handle of the chair—
we will travel along this life path until
one of us goes to heaven,
as the Lord continues to lead us along the way.

14

POETRY LIFE

After Ginny stepped into eternity, I prayed and asked the Lord for something new to work on. It was poetry. I was listening to *The Writer's Almanac* with Garrison Keillor. I started writing poetry in October 2015. This gave Ellen and I the spark to write poems of our own.

Poetry

Poetry is beautiful—
what a joy!
On our own,
the Lord has given us
new things to write about and share.

To quote the late Paul Harvey, "And now, the rest of the story."
This is what we are doing now. We are now active at First United Methodist Church. We are in the choir, and Ellen is able to sing in there because there is a lift that will take her up to the choir loft and back down. She is happy about that because she never had that before. Listening to her singing is music to my ears.

Music to My Ears

To hear my beautiful wife, Ellen,
so happy,
to use her vocal gifting,
to the glory of God.

As a liturgist, I am now reading scriptures every Sunday morning at church. We are members of the New Mexico Poetry Society. We also read in Poetry Fixed and Free, which is an open-mic poetry group that features local poets. We are also in the NMSVBI which is New Mexico School for the Blind and Visually Impaired.We will be having a website running very soon. You will also find a list of what we have there such as our mission statement, some of our past shows (which you can hear at any time), a contact page, and more. It is very blind-friendly. It has pictures, and it has a white background. We also have an inspirational phone line called Celebration and Praise Radio. It is 877-820-6261. The greeting will explain itself. We have a poetry book out. It is called *Variety of Original Poems* by Joe and Ellen N. Sorenson. And now we are writing this book.

15

◆◆ ◆ ◆◆

GOALS FOR THE FUTURE

This is what I have in mind for the future. I want to do more motivational speaking to talk about my story and promote my book. I will still continue to do the poetry and the other stuff. To reach me, call 505-554-1209 or you can e-mail me at joesorensen3@comcast.net.

Thank you so very much. We will end my story with some poetry.

Poems by the Sorenson's

RED BALLOON

A child is crying, crying,

"I want a red balloon,

please, please."

A woman said,

"My child, my child,

stop your crying—

here is a bowl of fruit with a red balloon."

—Joe Sorenson

SELF-PORTRAIT

1975 radio—

he was working at the control board

at KUOM Radio,

in Minneapolis, Minnesota.

He knew the control board very well;

my, my, why was he still in there?

The station manager

is not willing to hire him.

It is now 10:25 a.m.

5 minutes to radio station sign on,

the chief announcer walks in, saying,

"How would you like to go on the air at 10:30 a.m.?"

So he went on the air.

—Joe Sorenson

MY HEART

My heart rejoices

in the music of J. S. Bach.

Yesterday,

when I was feeling blue,

the music of George Frideric Handel lifted me up.

Let's put a handle on it—

when I am hungry, my heart longs for baked chicken.

Oh my, oh my, my heart leaps for joy for chocolate cake!

—Joe Sorenson

IF A FOOTBALL COULD TALK

If a football could talk,
it would say lots:
it would vent,
it would sound off,
it would say things like,
"I get abused all the time—
I get thrown around,
I get kicked around,
I get carried around,
I get fumbled and more.
I don't mind most of the time,
but all the time?
Make up your minds, please."

—Joe and Ellen N. Sorenson

ALABANZA

Alabanza—praise the mother who gave birth to her

even though she didn't want her

in 1929!

Praise the father whom I know nothing about.

Praise the twin brother who could see.

Praise the rest of the family whom, in spite of the fact that Ginny was

blind,

she prospered.

Praise the one who taught her massage and gave her a chance to learn

and make some money.

Praise the husband who saved her from losing it.

Praise her teachers who taught her how to read and write braille.

Praise all her caregivers, including me, who cared for her 'til the end.

—Ellen N. Sorenson

SPENDING TIME WITH FAMILY

At Christmastime in Alamogordo,

visiting with my stepsisters and my stepmother,

making different kinds of candy—

fudge with and without nuts,

peanut butter fudge,

toffee, and more—

chopping the nuts,

when it is either cooking or baking,

you could smell it all over the house.

It is a beautiful time with family.

At a restaurant with family,

the salsa and chips on the table,

my stepfather wanted a bowl of salsa to himself.

The rest of us laughed so hard because we know that he likes it hot.

He got it.

—Ellen N. Sorenson

CAREGIVING

Caregiving is hard work.

It takes a lot of patience.

It is a 24/7 job.

It takes a team to take care of the one that you love.

It takes a big heart to do it.

It can last a long time—

caregiving.

—Ellen N. Sorenson

THE DORM AT SCHOOL

It was during my years at NMSVH.

I had two different types of bathrooms that I used.

One had two stalls, a shower, and two doors.

Later on, I had my own bathroom, with a sink, a toilet, and a shower.

Both of them had a window at the top.

I had to share one of them with one other girl.

After I left school, due to the fact that I used a wheelchair, I had all

kinds of experiences in bathrooms—

for example, the ones that are never clean,

the ones that you can't close the door behind you,

the ones you can't get in to, the ones on a bus or a plane,

and the nice ones with all the space that you need.

—Ellen N. Sorenson

BLACK CAT

Oh black cat, oh black cat,

where are you at?

Writers have said mean things about you.

Oh black cat, oh black cat,

if I cross your path,

will you harm me in any way?

Black cat says, "No, no.

I won't do that,

I am a nice black cat."

—Joe Sorenson

CHRISTMAS JOY

Oh boy, Christmas joy—
lots of toys!
When I was just a lad,
I was so sad;
my mother was in the hospital
from an automobile accident.
Even at Christmastime,
the chimes rang out,
and to my surprise,
I received lots of tops—
all kinds of them,
small ones,
big ones,
ones that whistled,
ones that spun around—
oh, what fun!
Tuffy the cat liked them too;
he knew where they were at.
Christmas was joyful after all!

—Joe Sorenson

THE WRITER'S ALMANAC IS BACK

Oh boy, with great joy,

our e-mail inboxes are jumping with joy!

Once more, Garrison Keillor tells us of writers past and present,

he also tells us who is having a birthday that day and more,

And don't forget the poetry that he reads—

he also has a column that is a bonus for us!

We are now poets, thanks to him.

—Joe and Ellen N. Sorenson

BIBLE CAMP

Bible camp, once more with joy—
we were blind teenagers with our braille Bibles
and braille hymnbooks.
We studied and sang praises to His name,
and now the fun part—
because we were blind,
that didn't stop us from
swimming,
boating,
water skiing,
and hiking through the woods.

—Joe Sorenson

THE BEGINNING OF SUMMER

It is the beginning of summer:

The birds are singing,

the sun shines nice and bright,

it is also getting hot, and

we have waited all winter for this.

This is nice—

time to get out the lawn mower

and make lots of noise with it

while you clean up the yard

and do some gardening.

Happy summer!

—Ellen N. Sorenson

BASEBALL SEASON

It is time to bring out the bats and baseballs,

and play catch with your kids,

and attend a baseball game with friends—

it is time to eat hot dogs and take in all the fun,

so play ball!

—Ellen N. Sorenson

Riding on a Pony

When I was a child,
I liked to ride, ride
the little pony in the park—
oh, what a spark of joy,
to ride it.

—Joe Sorenson

GOING ON VACATION

It is time to go on vacation,

Taking a plane,

To a land that we have never been before,

This will be fun,

We will get help at the airport,

And have a ride to the hotel,

There will be lots of things to do,

Like affiliate breakfasts and lunches,

Seminars,

The General session,

And more,

This will be fun.

—Joe and Ellen N. Sorenson

MICROPHONE

Oh microphone, oh microphone—where are you at?

The microphone said,

"Oh Joe, oh Joe, never fear, I am here.

I was with you in many radio studios,

on stages across the United States,

you were emceeing—

also some at Poetry Fixed and Free;

when you were on stage and at these other places,

people laughed

because they thought that you were going to fall

because you are blind.

You showed them."

—Joe Sorenson

BIRDS

The birds outside,

in the trees,

in their nests,

making their music,

singing happily.

Hi, birds—

we hear you,

we love to hear you,

you make us happy!

We hear you on KHFM in the morning,

we learn about you from the girls at Wild Birds Unlimited—

you are God's creatures!

—Joe and Ellen N. Sorenson

SUNRISE, SUNSET

How it is nice

to see the sun rise

in the morning.

How nice and bright

and warm in winter,

to keep us warm

and, at the end of the day,

to see it set

in the late afternoon.

—Joe and Ellen N. Sorenson

BREAKFAST

In a small kitchen,
a deep round bowl—
perfect for breakfast.
Putting cereal in the bowl,
filling it with water,
putting it in to the microwave for two minutes.
So is it going to be oatmeal?
Oh, my stomach,
I am so hungry.
Growling, growling—
you can hear the sound.
It is so loud.
Be quiet, it is coming.
Next comes the coffee
in a nice coffee mug,
a little heavy when lifting it.
The coffee is instant:
putting it in to the cup,
filling it with water,
putting it in to the microwave for one minute,
taking it out,
and setting it down on the counter to stir it
because it already has the sugar and cream in it.
Finally putting it all on the table, which is round, with two places
for us.

—Joe and Ellen N. Sorenson

RENOVATION

When you undergo a renovation of a building,

such as an apartment building,

you face many challenges.

The layout that you have always known changes.

You feel lost.

The management don' always tell you what you need to know—

at least, not right away.

At some point, you will know what you need to know.

Things get turned around;

the front gets blocked by a wall.

Don't worry—

it is not the border wall.

Also during this time,

you will have to move out for a short time.

That is a pain because you have to clean out

your stuff.

That can be a mess.

At least, you have some time to do it.

That is fine because in the end,

it is well worth it because it looks

better than it did in the beginning.

—Joe and Ellen N. Sorenson

TRIBUTE TO PETER

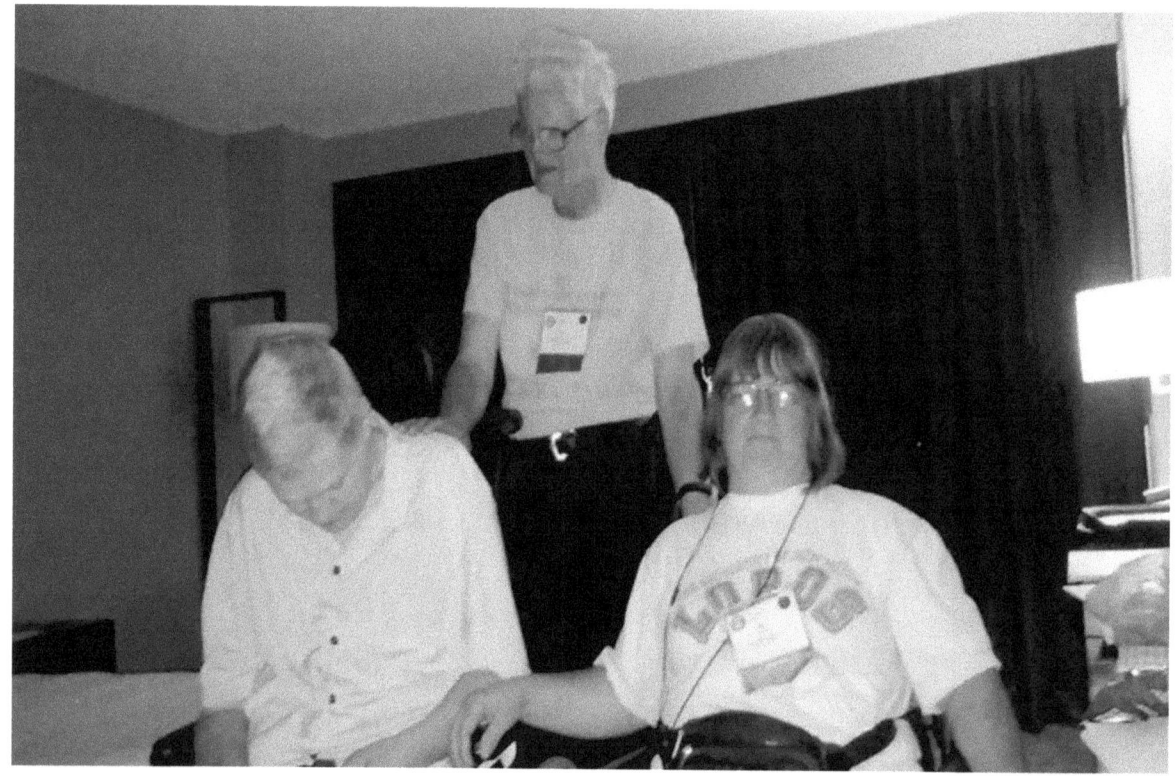

This is a tribute to my mentally ill brother, Peter, who passed away in August 25, 2017, and all the good care he received at the group home where he lived.

Peter, Peter, you were a great leader—

just like any other child you loved nursery rhymes.

One of them is "Simple Simon met a pie man."

At Christmastime, you loved the music;

you would say, "Christ the Lord."

When you became an adult,

you set the pace for others.

For example,

when our cousin, who was three years old,

wanted to pace the floor,

just like you.

But his mother said, "No."

At the group home,

everyone loved you,

but now you are loved in heaven.

—Joe Sorenson

IN MY HOMETOWN

In my hometown,

it was just like living in Mayberry:

Everybody knows everybody.

The town is so small;

you could walk from end to end.

The town is so small;

you could throw a rock from end to end.

You don't need a car;

it is not far.

So go forth and travel safe around town.

—Ellen N. Sorenson

ANGRY TV VIEWER

A man comes home from a long day's work;

he sits down on the couch,

to relax and watch some TV.

He turns it on, and what does he find?

Nothing but reruns on all the channels.

This makes him angry.

All he is thinking is,

Oh no, not again.

He wants to throw the remote

across the room,

but he don't

because he don't want to break it.

So he quickly puts it down

and turns it off.

What does he do next?

He reads a book.

—Joe and Ellen N. Sorenson

CHILDHOOD HOME

The house was in Alamogordo, New Mexico.

The address was 400 Sunrise.

It was in a cluster of streets,

with *Sun* as part of their name.

It was in a quiet neighborhood.

A three- bedroom house;

each bedroom a different color:

one was yellow,

one was purple,

the master bedroom was white,

and the den was where we watched TV.

One could access the kitchen from the den

or the living room.

Now someone else lives there—

two girls, six and a half years apart,

the youngest doing things by herself,

feeling all alone,

letting her imagination go,

being content—

just her parents and her.

Her older sister already out of the house.

That was when she was eleven years old.

—Ellen N. Sorenson

www.ingramcontent.com/pod-product-compliance
Lightning Source LLC
Chambersburg PA
CBHW041519120626
46551CB00018B/2499